Let's explore

Babies

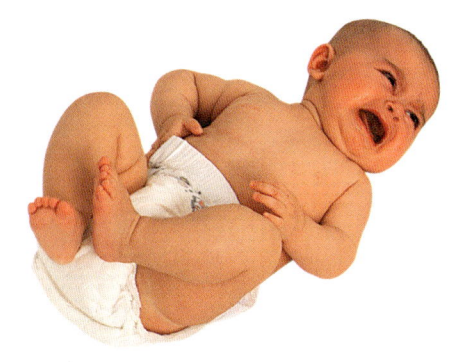

by Henry Pluckrose

FRANKLIN WATTS

Author's note

This book is one of a series which has been designed to encourage young readers to think about the everyday concepts that form part of their world. The text and photographs complement each other, and both elements combine to provide starting points for discussion. Although each book is complete in itself, each title links closely with others in the set, so presenting an ideal platform for learning.

I have consciously avoided 'writing down' to my readers. Young children like to know the 'real' words for things, and are better able to express themselves when they can use correct terms with confidence.

Young children learn from the experiences they share with adults around them. The child offers his or her ideas which are then developed and extended through the adult. The books in this series are a means for the child and adult to share informal talk, photographs and text, and the ideas which accompany them.

One particular element merits comment. Information books are also reading books. Like a successful story book, an effective information book will be turned to again and again. As children develop, their appreciation of the significance of fact develops too. The young child who asks 'Where did I come from, Mummy?' may subsequently and more provocatively ask, 'How did Daddy help you make me?' Thoughts take time to generate. Hopefully books like those in this series provide the momentum for this.

Henry Pluckrose

Contents

Being born	4
Pregnancy	6
New-born babies	8
We need to breathe	10
Caring for baby	12
Feeding baby	14
What do babies weigh?	16
Sick babies	18
Twins	20
Smiling and crying	22
Getting bigger	24
Talking	26
Animal families	28
Human families	30
Index	32

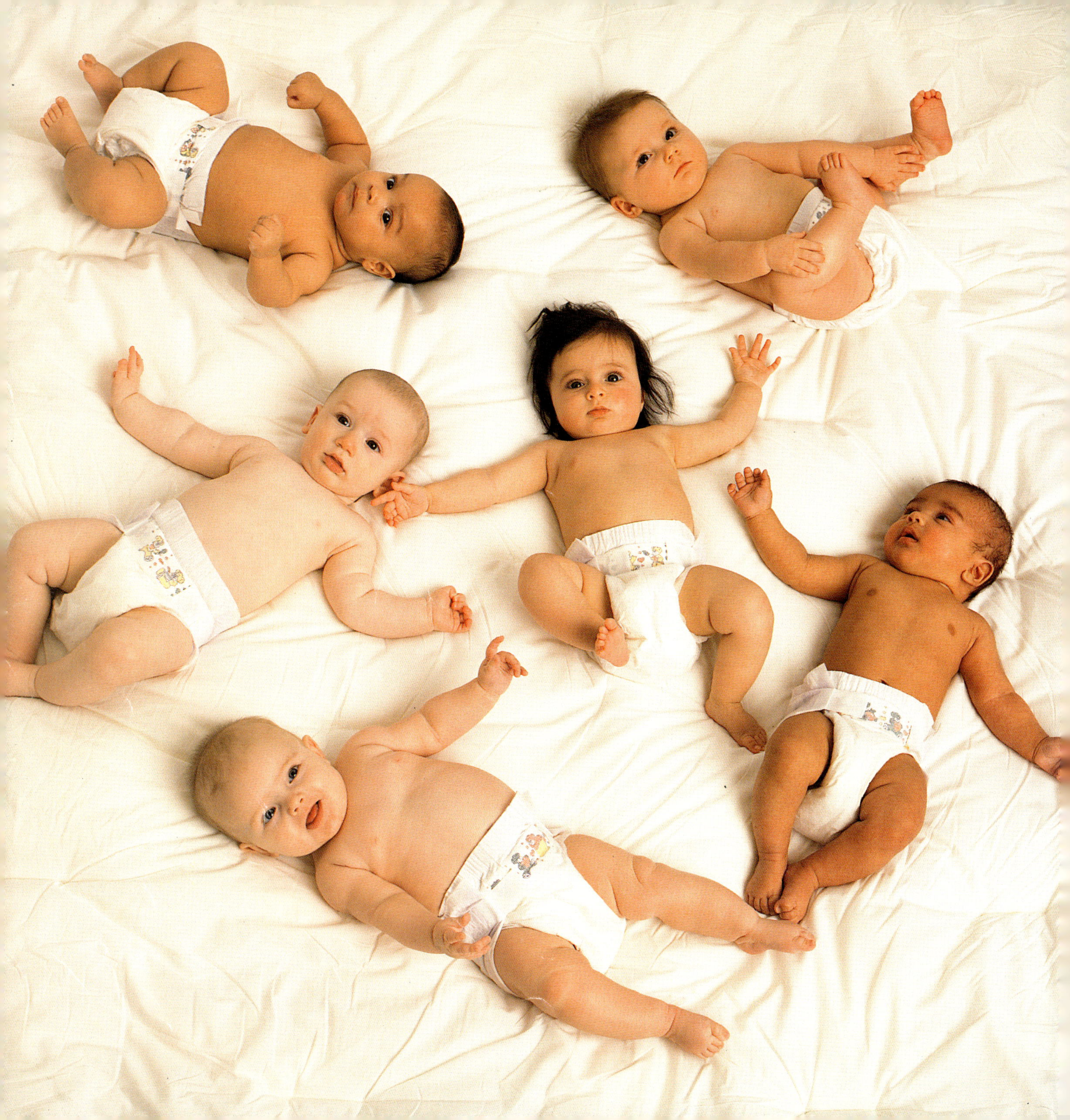

Every moment of every day,
every moment of every night,
somewhere in the world,
a baby is being born.

Before babies are born, they live and grow inside the mother's body for about 280 days. The mother's tummy. grows bigger: the baby needs room to grow.

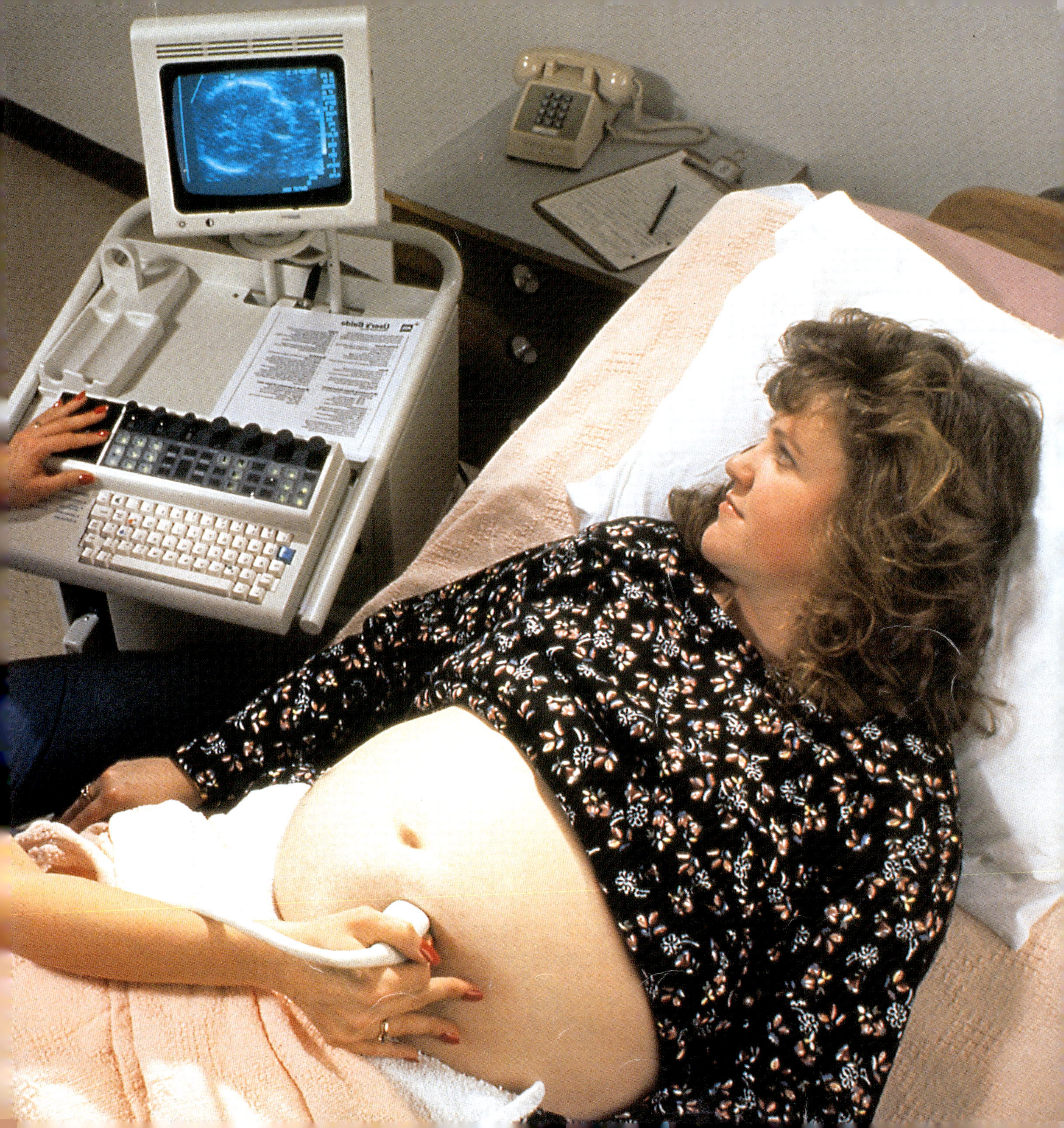

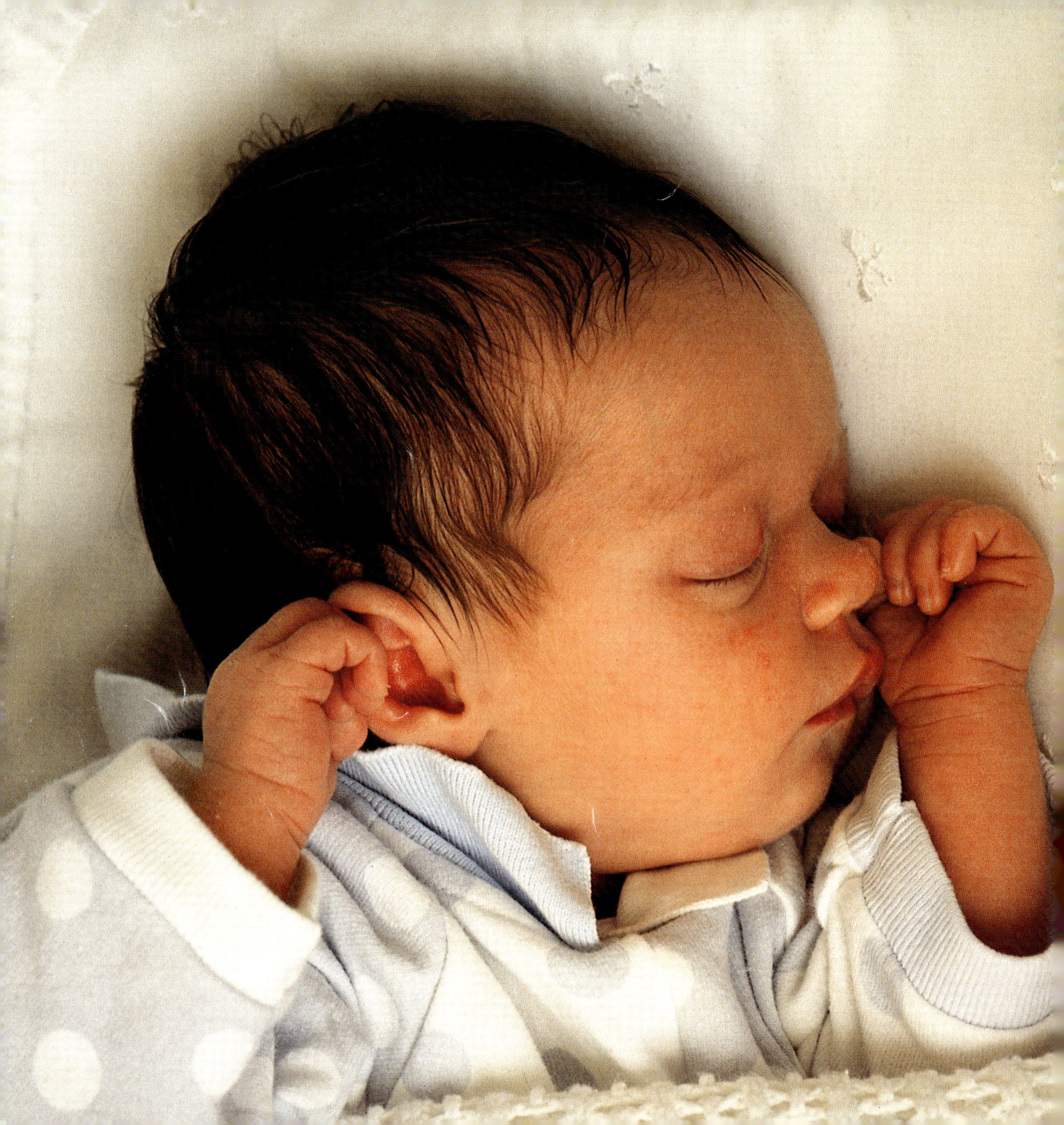

New-born babies are just like you.
They have eyes, ears, a mouth,
a nose, tiny fingers and toes,
and sometimes even hair.

The surprise of being born
makes the baby cry.
The baby takes oxygen
from the air and begins to breathe.

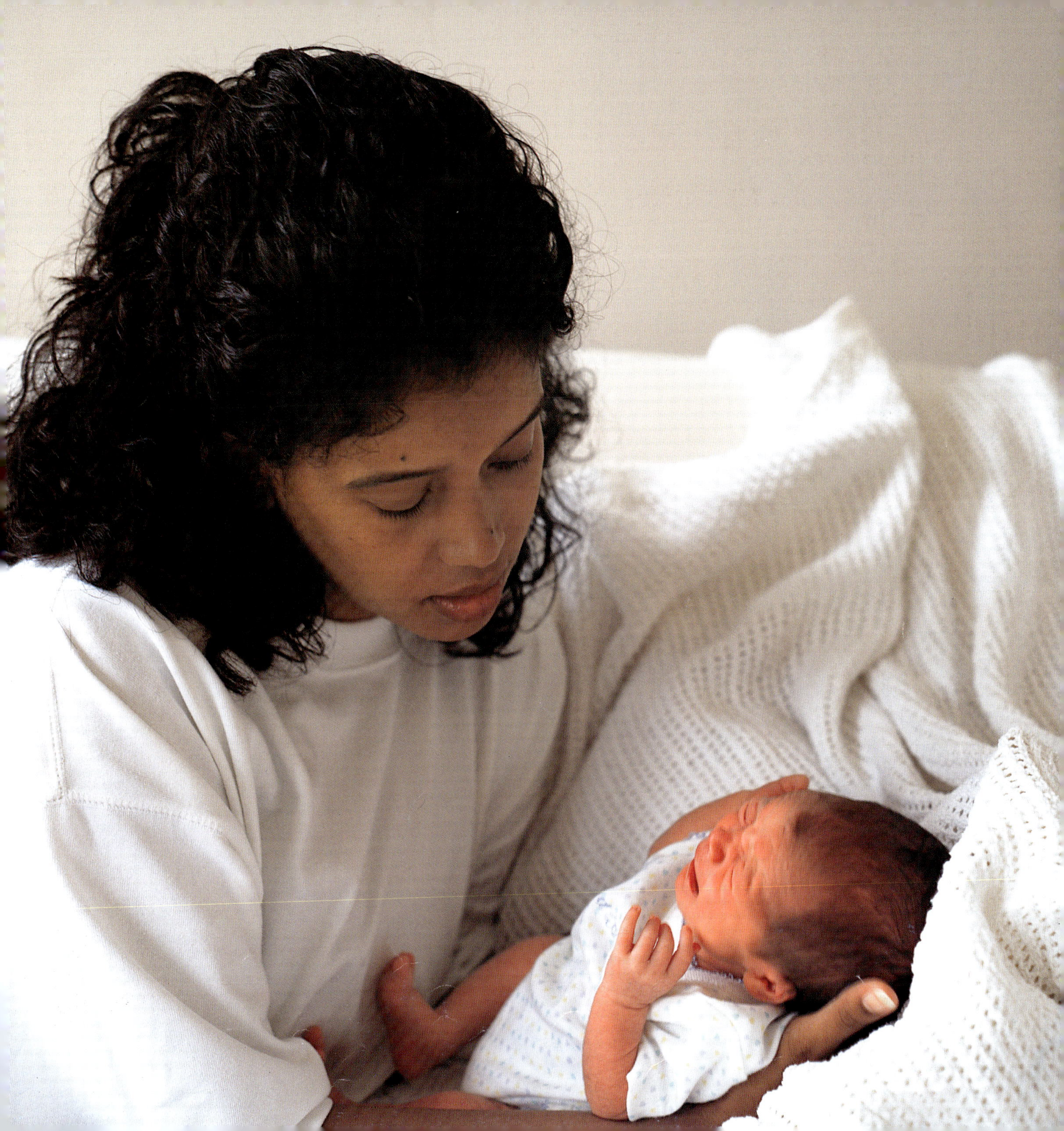

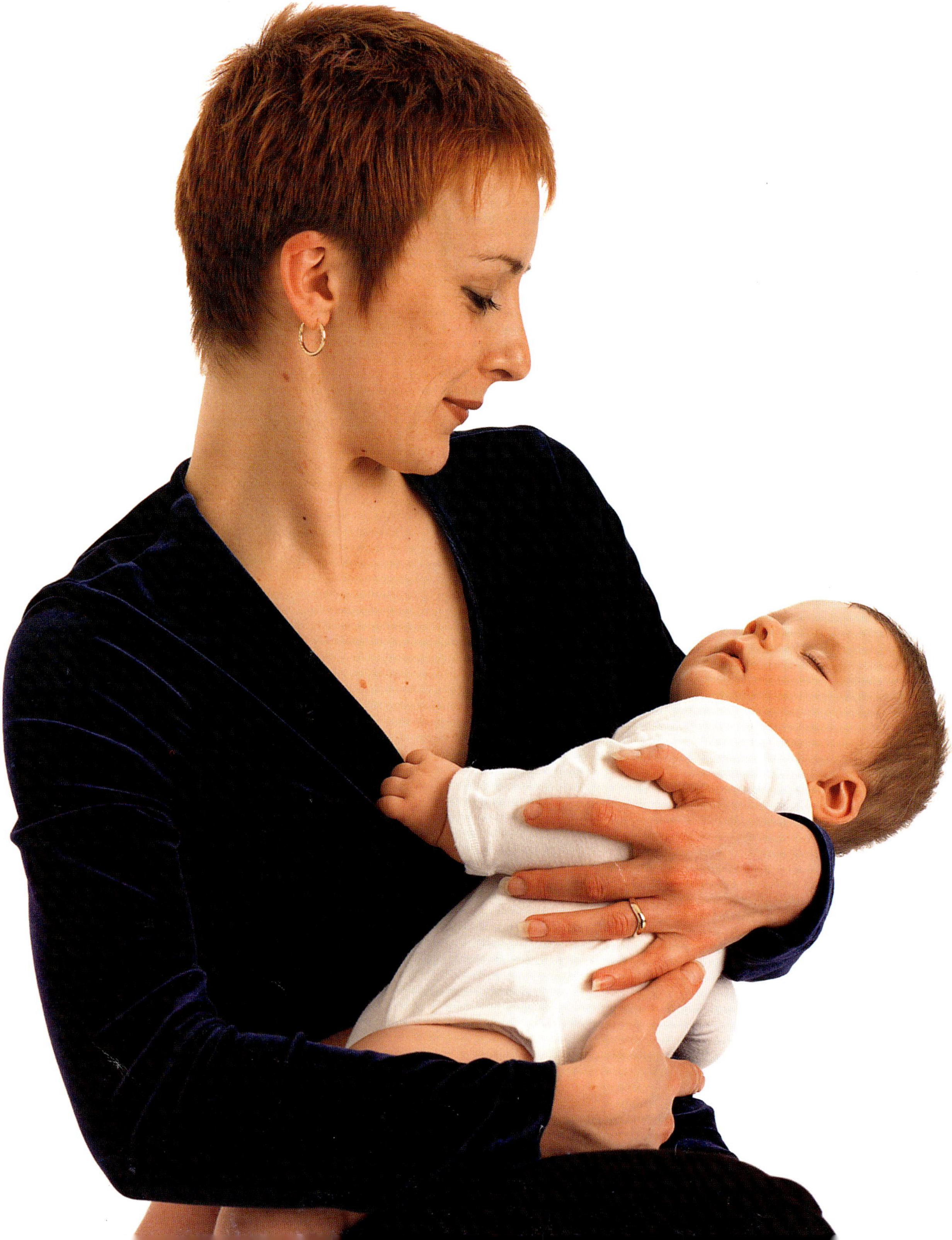

A baby needs food and warmth, sleep and love, just like you do.

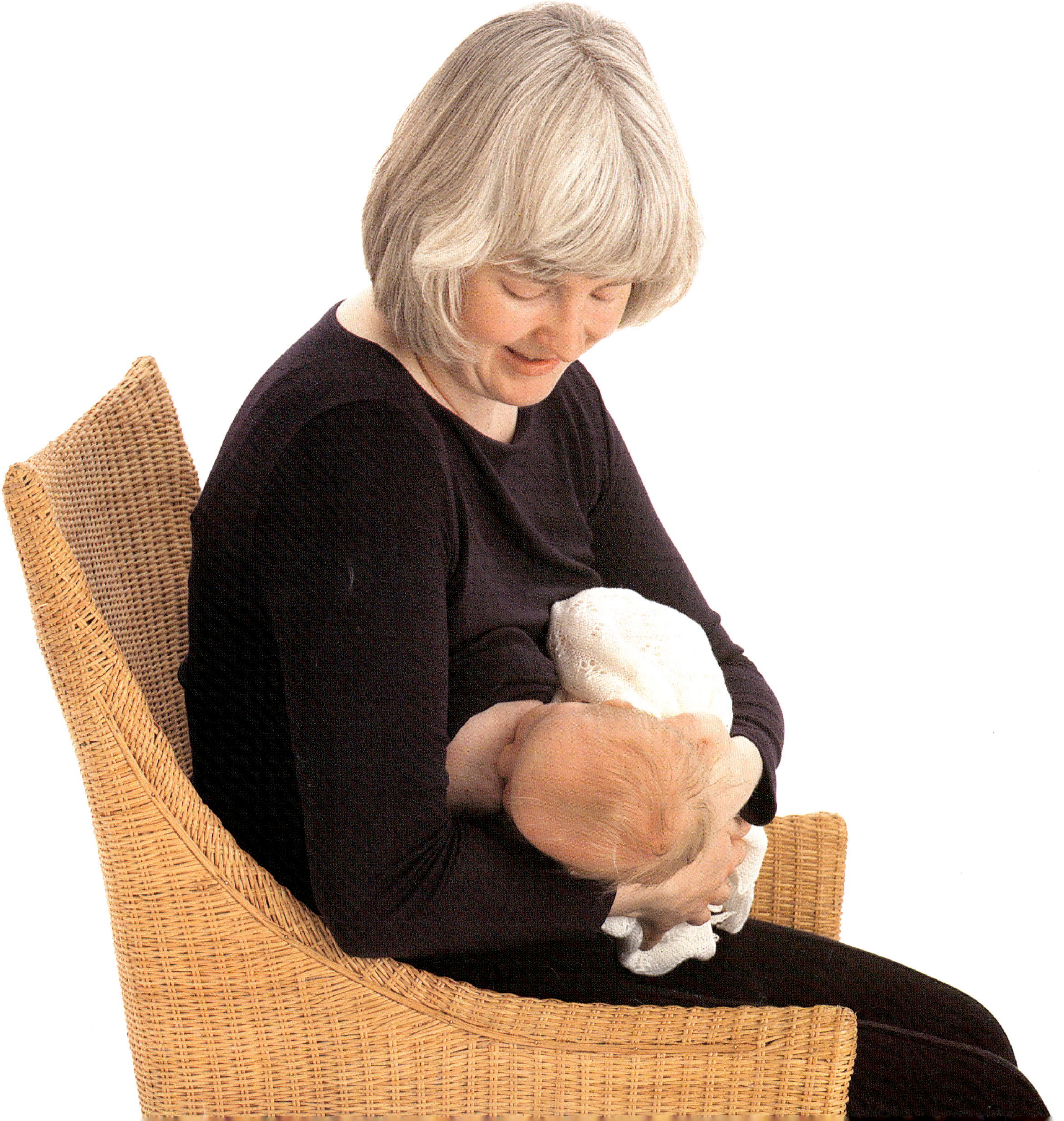

A new-born baby can only swallow liquid food. Milk from the mother is best. Sometimes, babies are fed with special milk from bottles.

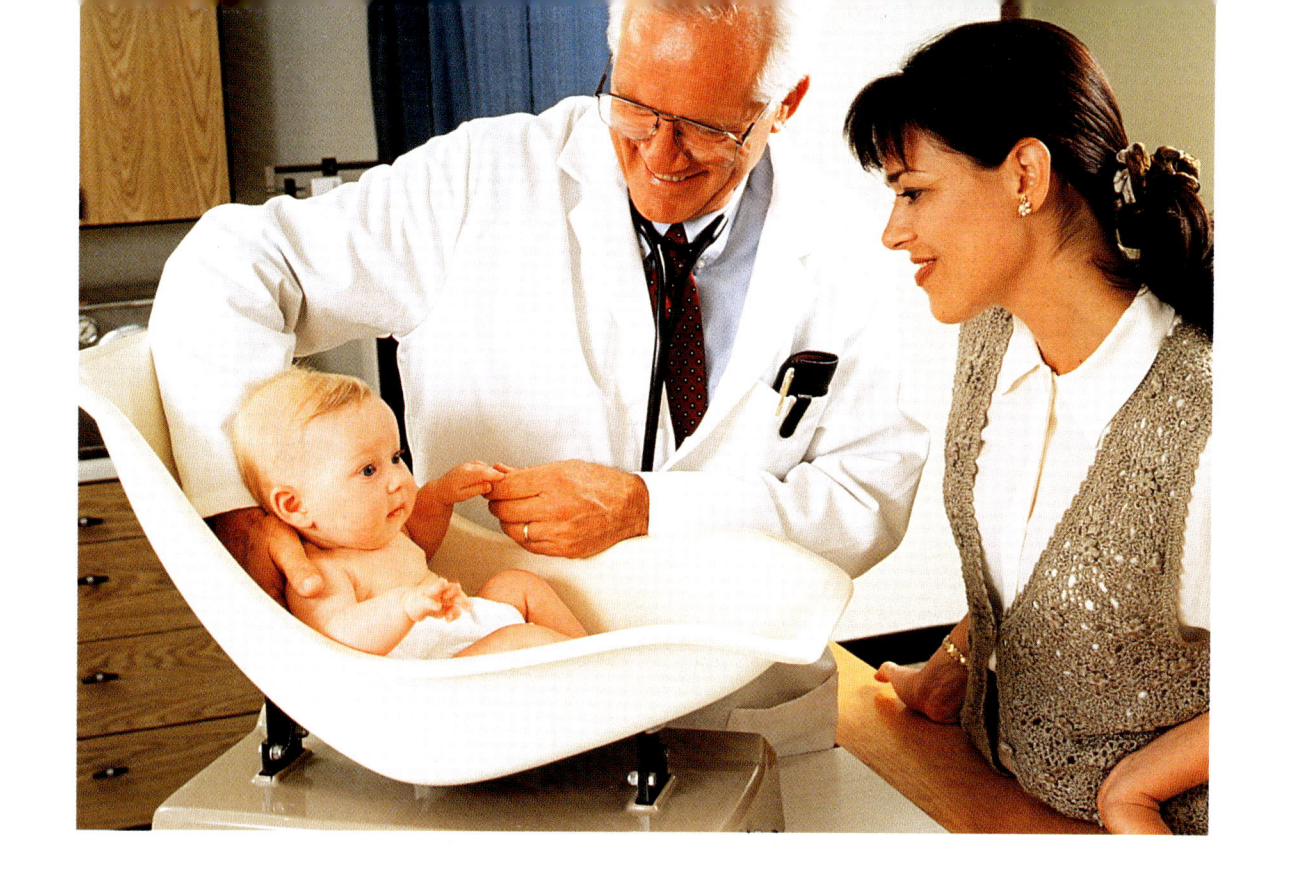

After babies are born,
they are weighed and measured.
How heavy were you
when you were born?

16

In poor countries, some babies are too small and weak to live.

In rich countries,
there are hospitals
to care for sick babies.
An incubator is a special cot
to keep babies warm,
and to help them breathe.

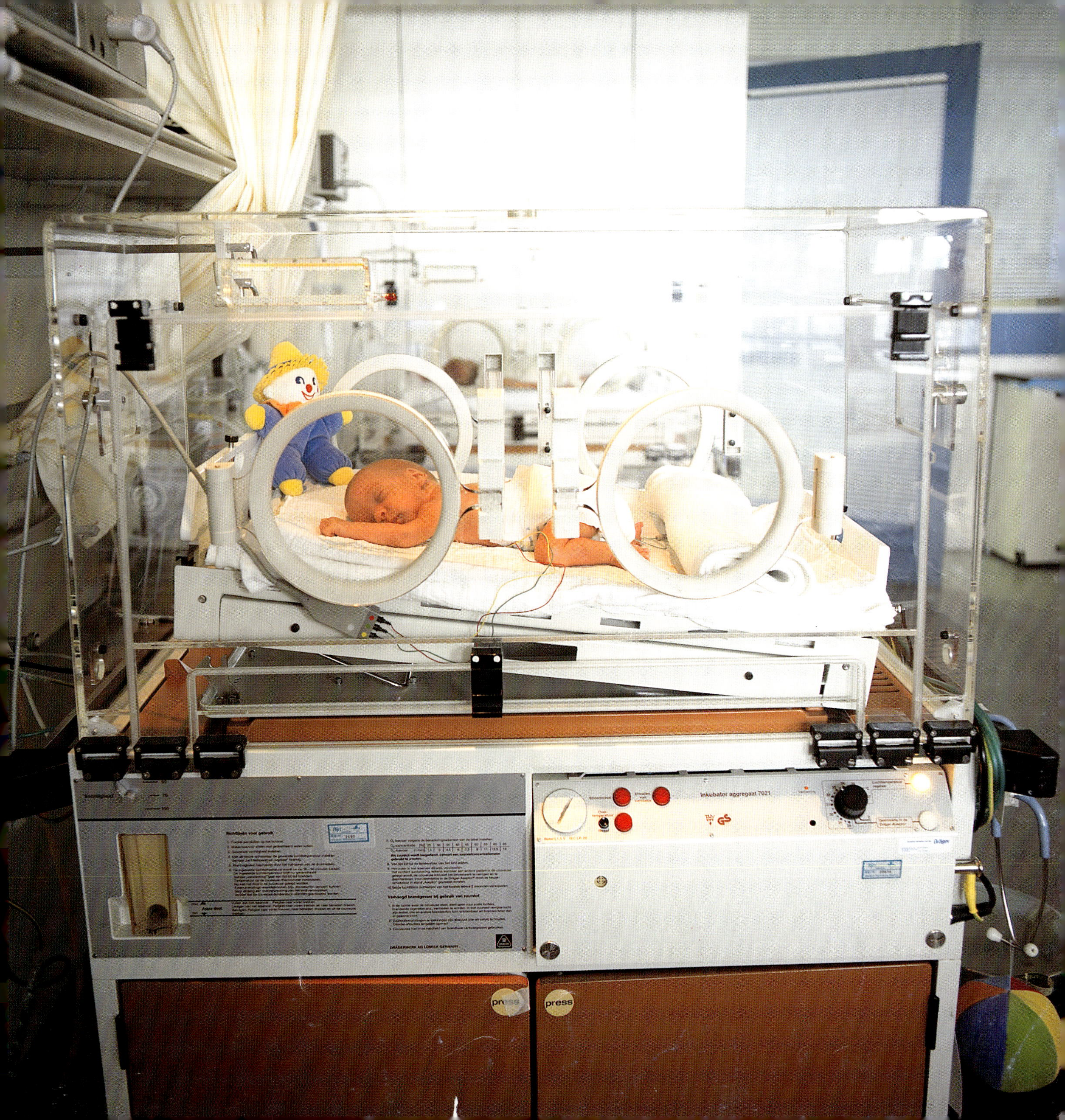
Inkubator aggregaat 7021
press
press

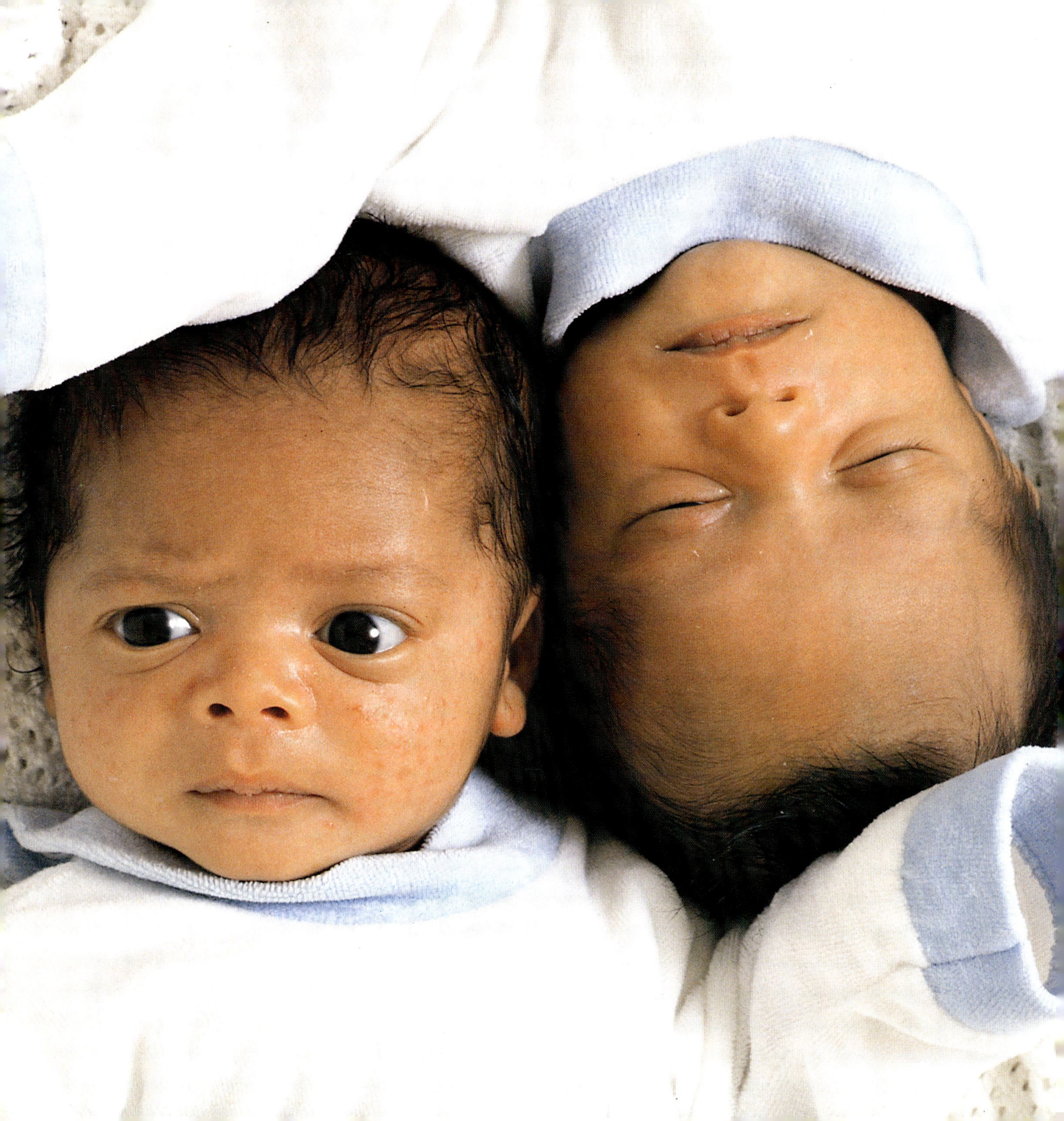

Sometimes, two babies grow
inside the mother's tummy
at the same time.
These babies are called twins.
Twins can look exactly the same,
or they can look quite different.

When you were small,
you could not speak.
You smiled when you were happy.
You cried when you were not.

23

Like all babies, you grew.
You began to make sounds.
You began to crawl.
You stood up and began to walk.

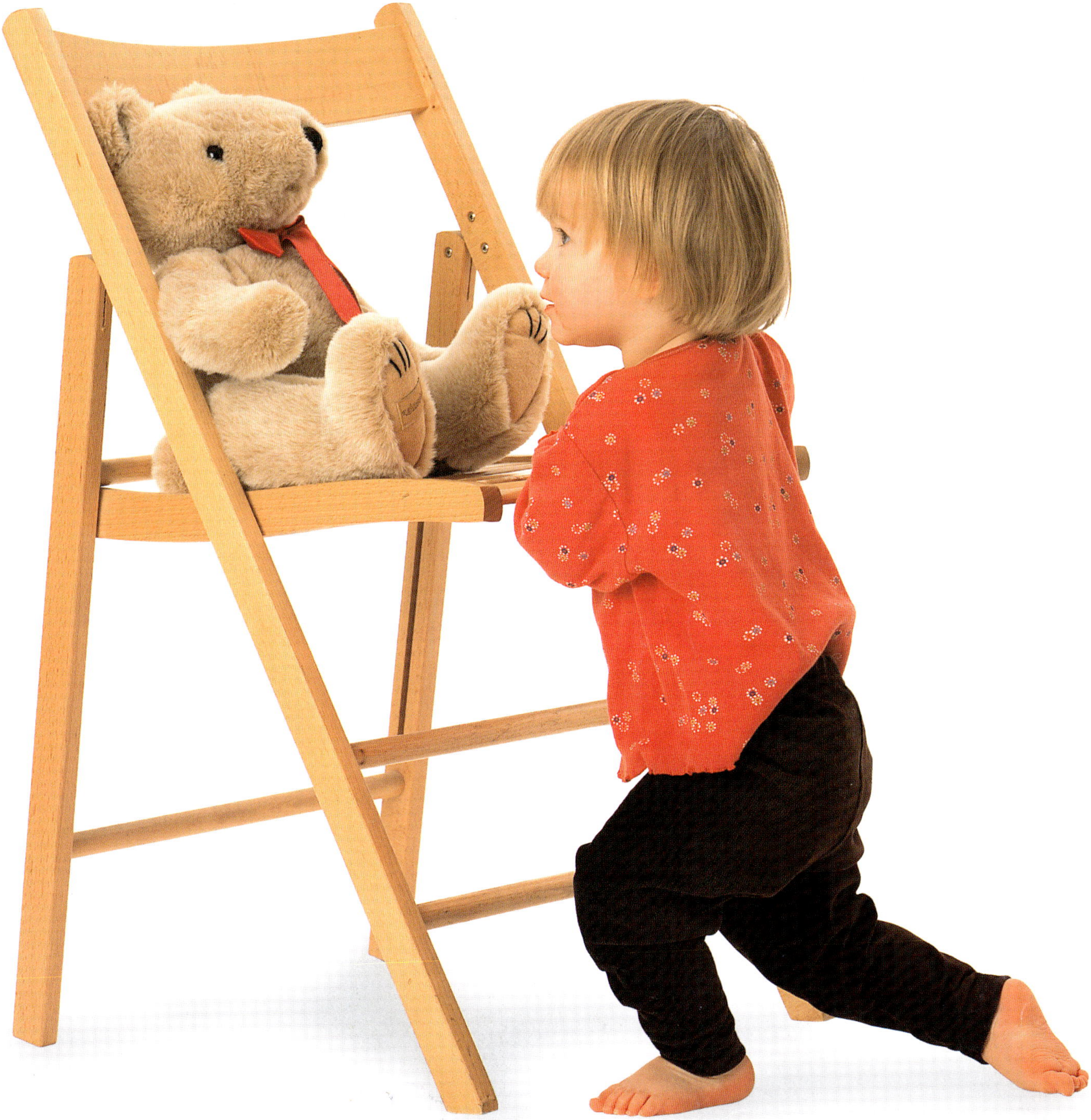

You copied the sounds
you heard around you.
Your baby babble became words.
Babies from different countries
make different word sounds.

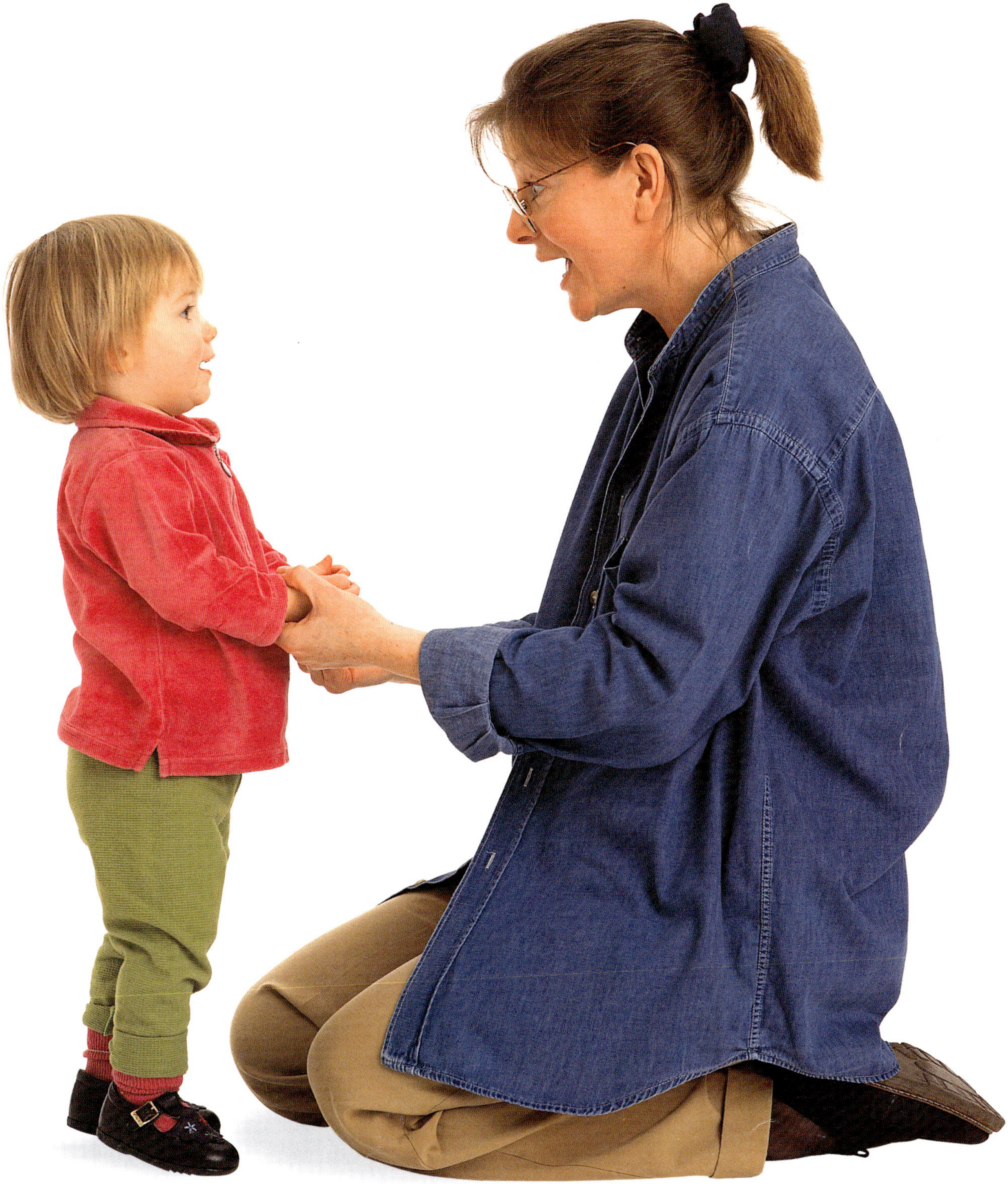

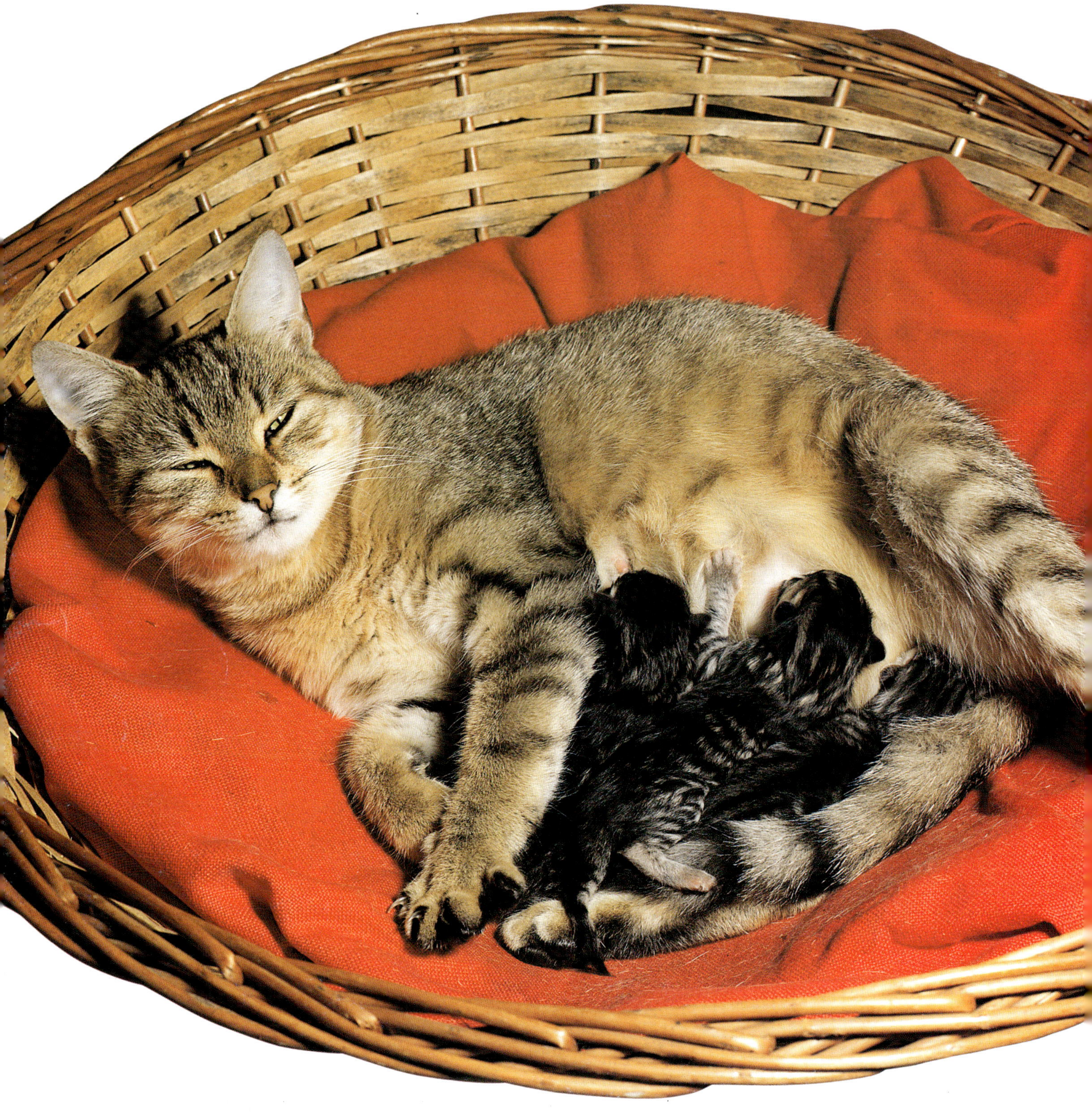

Animals have babies too.
Kittens grow inside the mother cat.
Kittens need food,
warmth and care,
just like human babies.

Human babies take many years
to grow into men and women.
When you have children,
do you think your mother
will like being called 'Granny'?

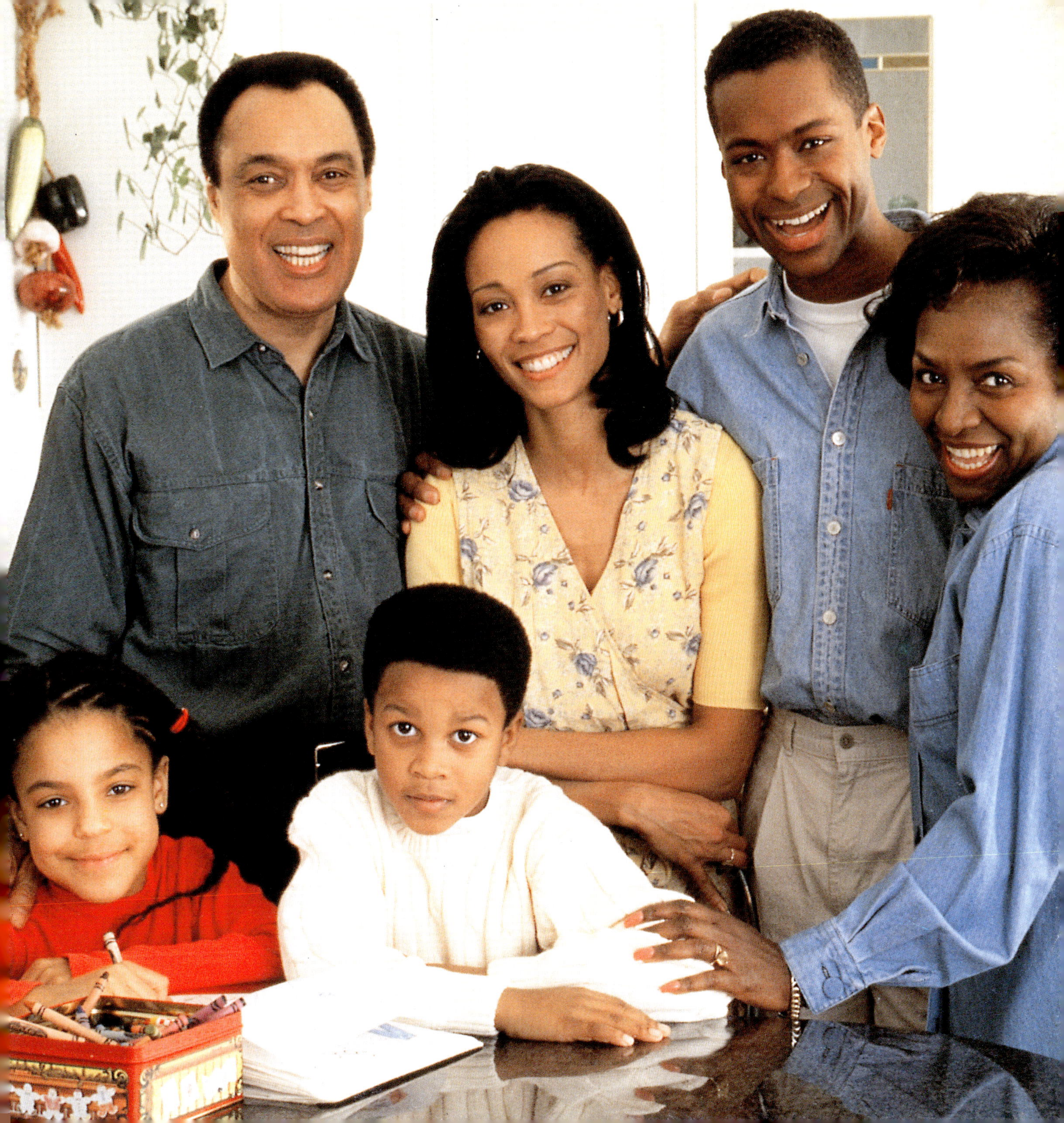

Index

animals 29

breathing 10, 18

children 30
crawling 24
cot 18
crying 10, 23

food 15

growing 6, 21, 24, 29, 30

humans 29, 30

incubator 18

love 13

measuring 16
milk 15
mother 6

oxygen 10

sleep 13
sounds 24, 26
speaking 23, 26

twins 21

walking 24
warmth 28
weighing 16

This edition 2003
First published in 1999 by
Franklin Watts
96 Leonard Street
London EC2A 4XD

Franklin Watts Australia
45-51 Huntley Street
Alexandria NSW 2015

Copyright © Franklin Watts 1999

Series editor: Louise John
Series designer: Jason Anscomb

A CIP catalogue record for this book is available from the British Library.

All rights reserved. No part of this publication may be reproduced, stored in a retrieval system, or transmitted in any form or by any means, electronic, mechanical, photocopy, recording or otherwise, without the prior written permission of the copyright owner.

Dewey Decimal Classification Number 649

ISBN 0 7496 5196 2

Picture Credits:
Steve Shott Photography pp. 4, 12, 14, 15, 22, 23, 24, 25, 27, cover and title page; Bubbles pp. 8 (Jennie Woodcock), 11 (Clarissa Leahy), 19 (Frans Rombout), 20 (Moose Azim); The Image Bank pp. 7 (HMS Images), 16 (Janeart), 31 (Nancy Brown); Robert Harding p. 17 (A. D Projects); Bruce Coleman p. 28 (Hans Reinhard).

Printed in Hong Kong / China